Compiled by
Roger Hardingham

The town of Weymouth is one of those special places in the wonderful county of Dorset. It has a great variety of outstanding features and has a fascinating past. Today, Weymouth is a leading seaside resort and is as vibrant as ever.

This brief guide to the town is not meant to be a full history or detailed account of Weymouth's past, but a pictorial tribute to its stunning waterfront and beaches, historic buildings, intriguing streets and royal connections.

Early records show that the Romans were present in the area soon after AD43. They sailed their galleys up the River Wey to Radipole where they could unload supplies for transport to the Roman Town of Durnovaria, now Dorchester, a few miles to the north. Long before the port was developed into what we see today, there were two towns. Melcombe Regis and Weymouth were great rivals on either side of the Harbour area. Melcombe Regis encompassed the Radipole area and where we now have Weymouth's main shopping area. Weymouth was on the western side and where the Trinity Road area is today. The harbour is still a crucial aspect of Weymouth. The quay tramway line to the ferry terminal no longer pays host to the Channels Islands Boat Express from London and the tracks have have gone from the streets since 2020. Fishing craft are also a major feature in the harbour area with boats bringing ashore fish and crabs for the lucrative local marketplace.

Weymouth's regal connections were endorsed by the regular holiday visits of King George III from the late 18th century. He loved dipping his feet into the refreshing English Channel waters off Weymouth. 'Mad' King George spent many weeks convalescing in Weymouth after he became very ill. His final holiday in Weymouth ended in 1805, coincidentally the year of the Battle of Trafalgar.

The arrival of the Great Western Railway to Weymouth in 1857 really put the town on the map. This, with memories of a regular royal visitor and good communications via the new railway from London, saw the seaside town of Weymouth become one of the most popular Victorian holiday destinations.

The Seaside Town

THE waters in the bay off Weymouth are the 'jewel in the crown' of the location. The English Channel brings in the warm currents of the Gulf stream along the Jurassic coastal area. Weymouth is right in the heart of it. It makes bathing, fishing, diving, sailing and all the other many water sports such a feature of the area. Seaside holidays in the town began to take off in the 1770s in Britain's 'first' seaside resort. With appalling conditions in many towns and cities in Britain, the privileged were to find great comfort from 'taking to the waters' in places such as Weymouth and dipping their feet into the sea.

For over 150 years, Punch & Judy shows have been part of Weymouth's soft sandy beaches. Today, 'Professor' Mark Poulton carries out daily performances in summer months.

Fact File

Weymouth has had a long association with holidaymakers. Since the arrival of King George III in the late 18th century for his holidays and the coming of the railways in 1857, people have flocked to the seaside town.

THE many colourful gardens in and around the town reflect the magic of Weymouth. Ever since the 1770s, the town has been a popular location for holidaymakers. A walk along the Esplanade will see views not only of the sea and beaches, but the well-kept gardens, cast-iron shelters and Georgian buildings along the whole sea front. The Victorians added the gardens at Greenhill and Alexandra and the Jubilee Clock in 1887 to honour Queen Victoria's Golden Jubilee.

Regular events take place throughout the year in the town. From War Veterans days, sailing events, specialist food fairs, beach ball games, kite flying and many more including the Carnival held in August which culminates with a firework display and often, weather permitting, a display by the RAF Red Arrows. The Pier Bandstand building is all that is left of a pier that was built in 1939. The pier itself was demolished in 1986 but the Art Deco main building survives with an amusement area and restaurant. The pleasure and stone piers are now the only places that reach into the bay.

Fact File

The Pier Bandstand originally had a pier out into the sea with an open-air theatre. The final remains were demolished in a spectacular fashion with a televised blast which saw the building crash into the bay!

HOW times have changed. Slightly over dressed children enjoy an age-old seaside tradition in riding donkeys on the beach at Weymouth in the 1920s. In many respects, Weymouth has retained its Victorian atmosphere with many activities on the beach in summer. You can still enjoy a donkey ride at the western end of the beach.

H.M. QUEEN VICTORIA
1887
H.M. QUEEN VICTORIA
1887

Royal Weymouth

THE royals started coming to Weymouth from as early as 1758. With the town firmly put on the social map of England, the Duke of York, George III's brother was entertained by quarry owner Ralph Allen. From the 1770s developers moved in and started building accommodation for the up and coming town and its visitors. Despite Weymouth's distance from Britain's major cities, it was by now served by regular mail and passenger coach services which made access a great deal easier than previously.

The new attraction of Weymouth and its health benefits attracted the Duke of Gloucester to build his own residence on the seafront. Known as Gloucester Lodge or Royal Lodge, it began a period of Royal visits to the town. Between the years 1789 and 1805 it became a regular haunt of King George III himself who was told to take 'the waters' off Weymouth to help cure his illnesses. The regal parade of buildings are shown below.

Some fascinating buildings survive from the Georgian period. The 'round houses' between St Thomas and St Mary streets form an amazing backdrop to the Kings Statue erected to mark George III's Weymouth connection. The King departed from Weymouth for the last time in October 1805 just as Admiral Lord Nelson was assembling his fleet, which two weeks later saw the defeat of the French and Spanish at the Battle of Trafalgar. The Kings Statue was completed in 1810.

Fact File

Bathing machines were used to take King George down into the water opposite the royal summer residence.
You can see a preserved example of a bathing machine in front of the Kings Statue.

IT'S easy to see why King George and his family enjoyed Weymouth. These fine golden sands form much of the beach area from the harbour side right over towards Overcombe. Traditional seaside amusements cover some of the beach, such as swinging horses, round-abouts and children's activities.

The Pavilion Theatre (left) is one that was built in the late 1950s after the previous 1908 building was completely destroyed by fire in 1954.

THE HARBOUR

ONE of Weymouth's little gems is its harbour. Connecting the old towns of Weymouth and Melcombe Regis is this lifting bridge, known as the Town Bridge. A bridge has been at this location for 350 years; this structure replaced an older crossing in 1930

The scene below shows a busy period in the harbour with the great Condor Seacat during its layover from Channel Island's duties and the ferryman crossing the harbour with a boat full of customers over to the Nothe. Weymouth's yacht club and several sailing boats are seen on across the harbour. This area was once a yard and slipway maintaining Cozens' paddle steamers.Since this view was taken, Weymouth has lost all its Channel Island's srvices.

SMALL fishing boats and trawlers form a major part of harbour life in Weymouth. These boats will often depart early in the morning and sail over to the southern tip of Portland to bring in their catches. The unloading creates a spectacle for onlookers along the quayside.

Fact File

The Town Lifting Bridge was opened by HRH The Duke of York on 4th July 1930. The bridge is a 'bascule' design and links the old town of Weymouth with Melcombe Regis.

VIEWED from Trinity Road is a busy harbour with fishing vessels of all descriptions. Catch of the day is landed. Dozens of crabs are caught off Weymouth and Portland and brought ashore for sale in local fish markets or for use in local restaurants. You can hire a day's line fishing, which is now an important trade in the harbour.

FACT FILE

Many buildings along the quayside once associated with the import of Channel Islands' produce such as potatoes, tomatoes and flowers have now been made into leisure amenities. By the 1970s imports of perishables had all but disappeared.

WEYMOUTH'S inner harbour area, the backwater, was developed from a working area for businesses involved in the repair of fishing and passenger vessels to the swish yachting marina of today. Hundreds of yachts and motor cruisers now line up within the spacious area. All have access to the open sea via the town's lifting bridge which is operated every two hours at peak times. A strict speed limit is enforced.

LOOKING north towards the town. The long quayside has changed dramatically over the years with the Great Western Railway passenger ships and goods vessels no longer berthing to load and unload their passengers and cargo.

The harbour is now more commonly used for leisure purposes apart from the fishing vessels.

Occasional large sailing vessels can be seen along the quay, such as the *Pelican of London* which is a sail training ship operated from Weymouth.

Weymouth has the dubious distinction of being the port where the plague, or black death, came into Britain in 1348. From its beginnings in Melcombe Regis the plague quickly spread over the whole region and eventually all of Britain killing an estimated 30-50% of the whole population.

Prices have changed for the ferry across the river since this photograph!

THE quayside is a transformation of previous times. Gone are the warehouses once used for the Channel Islands trade and gone have the old tracks of the quay line.
The scene below shows steamers being prepared for their next crossings. The first vessel in view is the cargo ship *Pembroke.*

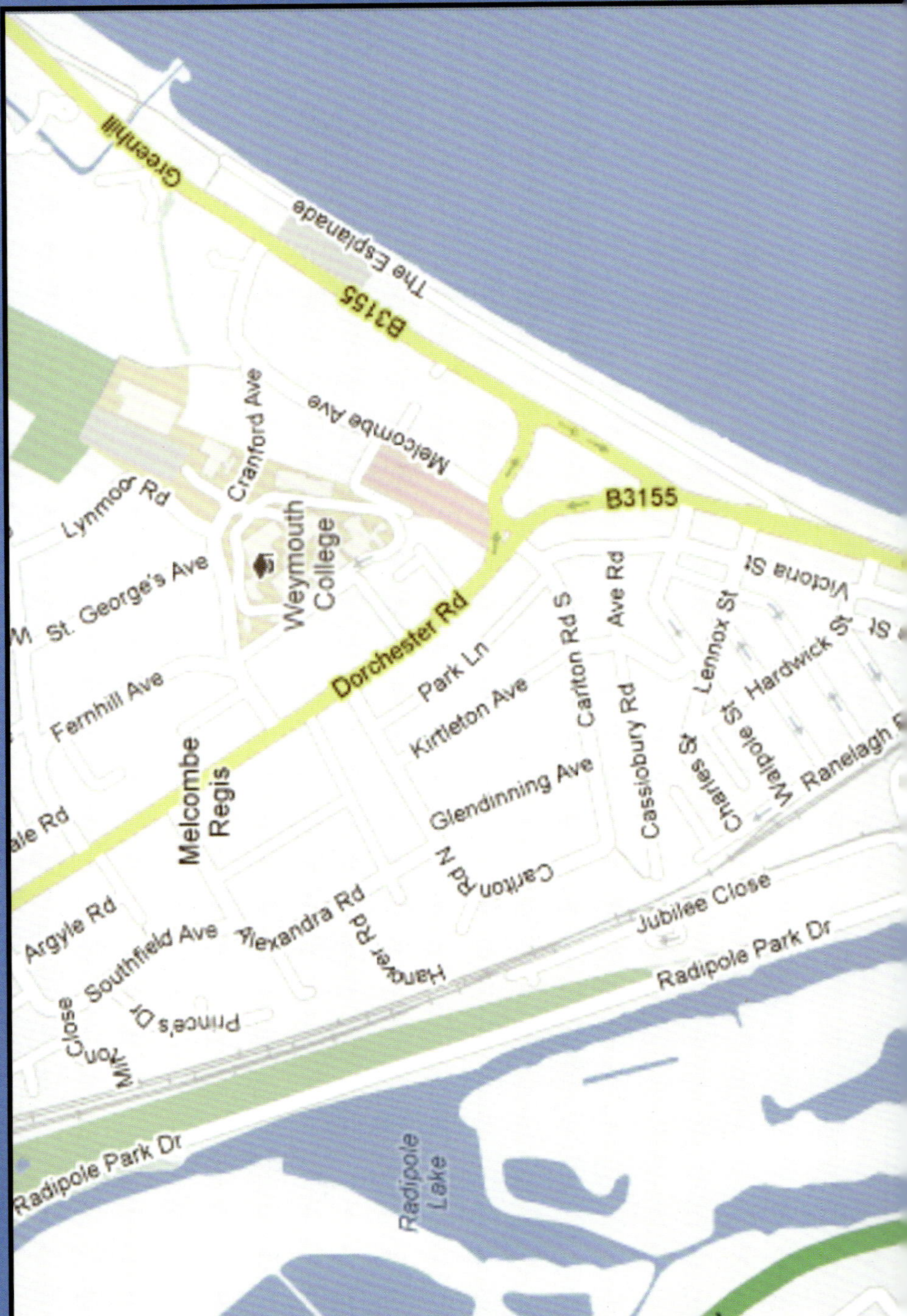

Greenhill
The Esplanade
B3155
Cranford Ave
Melcombe Ave
Lynmoor Rd
Weymouth College
St. George's Ave
B3155
Victoria St
Ave Rd
Dorchester Rd
Carlton Rd S
Lennox St
Hardwick St
Park Ln
Kirtleton Ave
Fernhill Ave
Melcombe Regis
Cassiobury Rd
Charles St
Walpole St
Ranelagh
Glendinning Ave
Carlton Rd N
Jubilee Close
Argyle Rd
Southfield Ave
Alexandra Rd
Hanover Rd
Radipole Park Dr
Prince's Dr
Close
Radipole Park Dr
Radipole Lake

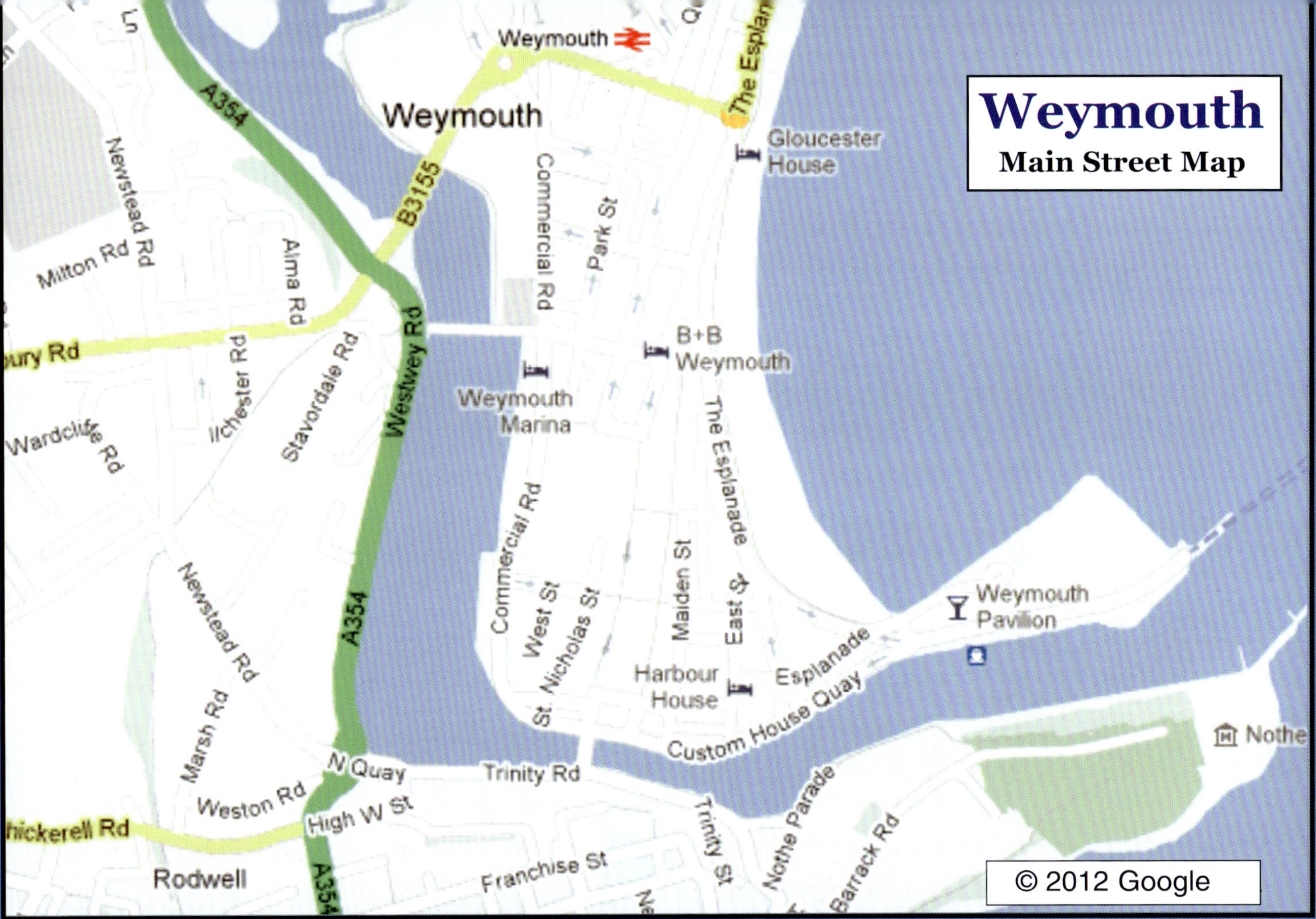
Weymouth
Main Street Map
Weymouth
Gloucester House
The Esplanade
B+B Weymouth
Weymouth Marina
Commercial Rd
Park St
West St
St. Nicholas St
Maiden St
East St
Harbour House
Esplanade
Custom House Quay
Weymouth Pavilion
Nothe
Trinity Rd
Trinity St
Nothe Parade
Barrack Rd
Franchise St
N Quay
High W St
Weston Rd
Marsh Rd
Newstead Rd
Rodwell
A354
B3155
Westwey Rd
Stavordale Rd
Ilchester Rd
Alma Rd
Milton Rd
Wardcliffe Rd
© 2012 Google

PART of the defences of the area. The Nothe Fort was built in the mid 1800s as part of the construction of the Portland Breakwater. This whole area which includes the Stone Pier is easily assessable from the harbour via the Nothe Parade. Some amazing views are available including the occasional arrival of the paddle steamer *Waverley* in the late summer.

Fact File

The Nothe Fort was completed in 1872 the same year as the Portland Breakwater. It was armed with four 9-inch and six 10-inch guns which were never actually fired in anger. The Fort is well worth a visit.

THE Victorian-built Fort at the Nothe is now a museum and visitors' centre showing how Weymouth was involved in the defence of the nation. The Portland Breakwater (below) is seen clearly here. When the Royal Navy was based here, the fleet would often be seen moored in the 'Portland Roads'. The Nothe Gardens are in the foreground and the Isle of Portland in the distance behind the breakwater.

ANOTHER fortification in the area is Sandsfoot Castle. The remains of the castle stand over the Portland Roads which is why Henry VIII had this and the one at Portland built in the 16th century. It is thought the stone used for its construction came from near Wool.

About two miles east of Sandsfoot is Greenhill with its colourful gardens, tennis courts, bowling green and cafes. The weathervane is a tribute to local aviator G. H. Stainforth who became the fastest man to fly during the Schneider competition of 1931 in the Solent.

WEYMOUTH is about holidays and fun. The large complex of buildings set on the hillside west of the town at Bowleaze is the Riviera Hotel. This dates from the Art Deco period of the 1930s and was also used during World War II as a hospital. During the 1950s Pontins took it over as part of their holiday camp network. It is now a large hotel and restaurant under new ownership. As well as surfing and sailing, hang gliding is a popular sport in the area which gives spectacular views of the Jurassic Coast for participants.

Fact File

The Jurassic World Heritage Site provides a complex mix of geological forms. Much of the coast east of Weymouth has clay, limestone and sandstone. Often, traces of oil can be seen in the sea off Osmington Mills.

NATURE is very close to the centre of Weymouth. The River Wey broadens out into Radipole Lake where the RSPB Nature Reserve is based. The view above is looking north with Westham Bridge crossing the Radipole Lake. There was once a railway bridge at this location which was the start of the branch line to Portland. This closed in 1965.

Left is a view along Commercial Road in 2012 eight years before all these old tracks were lifted and the road re-surfaced.This was the disused Weymouth Quay tramway which went all the way from Weymouth station down to the ferry passenger terminal in the harbour and used regularly by boat trains.

THE eastern extent of this guide looks at the white carved figure of a man and a horse at Osmington. This is in fact the figure of King George III which was sculpted in the limestone South Dorset Downs at Osmington in 1808. The whole figure is 280 feet in length and 323 feet in height. Various attempts have been made to clean up the white horse and in 2012 it was finally completed in time for Weymouth's part in the 2012 Olympics.

The view across Weymouth Bay looking towards Bowleaze and Osminton Mills. The whole of this 95-mile coastline from Old Harry Rocks near Swanage in the east over to Exmouth in the west was made a World Heritage Site in 2001.

BUILDINGS

WEYMOUTH is very much a Georgian town, but it also has a number of buildings that still survive from Tudor and Stuart times.Many old buildings have been demolished even in recent times such as magnificent Tudor houses along North Quay in the building of the new municipal offices in the 1960s!

Quaint and colourful terraces surround the harbour along Hope Street and Nothe Parade.

At the far end of this old photograph is the bell and clock tower of the Old Town Hall as built on the Weymouth side of the harbour in the Tudor period. The building survives today in what is now called High West Street and the ancient public house, The Boot Inn, also survives close by.

THIS terrace of houses, called Pulteney Buildings, dates from 1805 and is very much the Georgian look of Weymouth. The bow fronted windows are also to be seen in other streets such as Devonshire Buildings and Brunswick Terrace. Many of these houses have been turned into hotels and guest houses for visitors.

Below is the revamped Custom House Quay following the extraction of the old railway tracks from the road surface. Now a vibrant area with restaurants and bars.

VICTORIAN promenaders enjoy the Esplanade in a period with not a single motor vehicle in view. Horse-drawn taxis queue for business and you can just see some bathing machines at the waters edge on the right.

Left, the clock tower of St Marys Below, the distinctive building of the Harbour Master's offices.

ONCE a busy scene of engineering premises and paddle steamers being overhauled, the area around the Inner Harbour has been transformed into flats but still with moorings for fishing vessels and leasure yachts. The extensive marina is in the left background.
The very ornate Fish Market building of 1855 on the quayside survives today in the same business it started out as. Fresh fish, crabs, lobsters and other shell fish are sold here after being landed from the trawlers just across the road.

A quayside hoist frames the Old Weymouth side of the town which includes the old brewery and a collection of properties huddled around the outer harbour. To the right is one of the cafes on the Esplanade which was designed to resemble an up-turned hull of a boat.

Fact File

The New Rooms Inn pictured left is directly opposite the Old Rooms in Trinity Road. The Duke of Gloucester had tea in these rooms in 1771 when they were called the Assembly Rooms. Nowadays the Old Rooms is a pub and restaurant.

ONE of the most delightful areas of Weymouth harbour. Some bow-fronted houses along Nothe Parade are flanked by the Dive Center on the left and some later additional terrace housing. The once hectic port area which would have seen paddle steamers, Channel Island ferries and cargo vessels is now a more tranquil setting with more leisure boating and fishing.

REMEMBRANCE plaques in Weymouth recall the fallen residents from the two world wars. The main memorial is close to the Pier Bandstand at the eastern end of the Esplanade.The memorial was dedicated in 1921 following World War I and then subsequently names were added to it from World War Two fallen. The restored memorial was completed in 1997. Weymouth was heavily involved in the D-day operations of June 1944 when the port was transformed into a base for the dispatch of troops and equipment for northern France.

The memorial below is dedicated to the Australian Commonwealth Military Force, the ANZAC troops who passed through various training camps and hospitals in Dorset after seeing action at Gallipoli in 1915.

FACT FILE

World War II had a dramatic effect on Weymouth. The port area was commandeered by the military and all normal operations ceased. Over 500,000 troops embarked from Weymouth between June 1944 and May 1945.

Fact File

Fred Darrington started sculpting sand on Weymouth's seafront from the 1920s through to the 1990s after which Mark Anderson took over. Mark did a sculpture of Windsor Castle for the Queen's visit to Weymouth in 2009.

SCULPTURES in sand have been a part of Weymouth's Esplanade since the 1920s when Fred Darrington began the art of using sand and water to create anything from figures to buildings. Thesedays, his grandson Mark Anderson has continued the family tradition not only on the seafront, but at Sandworld in the Lodmoor Country Park. This is the first dedicated sand sculpture park in Britain. The technique requires the right amount of sand and water being mixed to create the workable mix for the various artists to create their masterpieces.

TWO very different maritime features of Weymouth. The town's lifeboat operated by the RNLI is named *Ernest and Mabel.* One of the Severn Class of lifeboats, it is moored in the harbour ready for any emergency.

The world-famous Chesil beach is viewed from the top of Portland. This spectacular geological phenomenon controls the way in which the coastal area around Portland and Weymouth has developed over millions of years.